REGULARS

REGULARS

Rit Chattapadhyay

Hawakal
PUBLISHERS
New Delhi | Calcutta

HAWAKAL
New Delhi | Calcutta

HAWAKAL PUBLISHERS
70 B/9 Amritpuri, East of Kailash, New Delhi 65
33/1/2 K B Sarani, Mall Road, Calcutta 80

Email info@hawakal.com
Website www.hawakal.com

Cover photo Shuttertock

Cover designed by Bitan Chakraborty

First edition (paperback) February 2022

ISBN: 978-93-91431-27-3 (paperback)

Price: INR 300 | USD 14.99

for
everybody in pain

We will Talk — an introduction to *Regulars*

It is challenging for me to write about *Regulars*. I will let the readers figure it out on their own. I believe they will. Instead, I'll write about the poet who composed the poems.

I wrote my first poem when I was 17. It was not an abreaction, but as Edward Bond says, it was the act of breaking the hold of ideology. As a young kid in a dusty school, I was constantly bullied. I was fat, unconfident, and vulnerable. I was made fun of and laughed at. I fell in love, and it did not work out like most love stories that begin in school. I was a misfit, and I think I remain the same. I am afraid of crowds, even if it includes people I know.

Out of sheer angst, I began writing what came to me. That year, which was possibly 2010, I wrote a lot. Within a swift period, my diary was filled with scribbles and scratches. This was me fighting back — my counterattacks. However, none of the poems you will read are from that time. Yet, those days have made these poems. The absences of those poems mark the presence of the poems you will read.

The poems in *Regulars* were written while I was studying English Literature and Language at the University of Calcutta, College Street Campus. I owe a lot to those lectures given by legendary professors in the Department of English. They gave me confidence, taught me about a world bigger than the narrow confines of middle-class mediocrity, and nurtured my imagination. These poems are also grateful to the numerous friends I made at the university. I raise a toast to them; I thank all the walks that I have taken alone or with somebody through the alleys and streets of this vibrant and empathetic city. Finally, I thank the numerous people I have met, whose names I do not know but have helped me grow.

Most of these poems are observations of life in motion, stagnant energy, and painful life. I believe that these poems are not pessimistic. They are optimistic. They are confident in observing (not crying over) the minutes we miss, the love we lose, and the time we fail to see going by us. These poems would love if they could help you, soothe you, or make you feel that someone out there knows what you are going through.

I am not good at writing prose, so I will see you around. And, we'll talk. Till then, take care and know you are beautiful.

Rit Chattapadhyay
7 Feb 2022
Calcutta

CONTENTS

between you and me!

ABIGAIL AND WINDOWS

Nights
when she comes
you can't breathe.

She
undresses the iron suit
dots of flesh deck the floor
creating a red-white pattern
insignificant yet arresting,
she leaves smiling.

Baba says to keep the windows open. I do it.
She can make me cry, again
till windows become leaves.

ABIGAIL: A DREAM

You control the mind all day to prevent
her return in form or shape
sound or steam, but
she comes back in a dream kissing you.
Lips that make life and death fly into mid-air
the air enters my penis, and I wake
up before Nightfall.

I had masturbated yesterday.

INTERVIEW 105876

When you think about writing some things
but
then
nothing comes to your mind, you think why
the sweat doesn't look any different from last month's,
women and men you had once loved
are fucking other people and
it does not really matter
she hops into your dream and back,
calling you an impotent for
things you can't control
the assholes from sweet neighbourhood
tinder through life endlessly
so
what has changed?
You've given a few interviews where they've asked
1. Describe yourself
2. Your strengths
3. Your weaknesses
We are just poets living in a van by the river, sir.
Had we known these answers
don't you think we'd rather be drinking ale with Norsemen
instead of wearing stupid formals into
your black garment store.

AFTER HER

I often wondered why I couldn't forget her.

With my newborn in hand and looking at my wife
smile, I realized
it was because she could leave me before I left her.

BLIND

Emotions in a pen-case
are covered with brown
paper, we never see it
always blind.
Always.

BLUE GOODBYE

We stood on a metal frame
posing nude for the first time.
A click later,
I saw her walking towards the city train
she was buying newspapers,
she walked right up to the edge
the train opened up and became a blue flower.
None of the other passengers could see us
we jumped into the flower.

She was the last of them
The last of them who could wonder.

MARKER

We have been loving pointers
all at the same time.

It becomes an inverted dream
and a white mark on the cloth.

Love is just a type of intimidation
a bluff of delicate needles,
the non-sequitur
in images of each other.

PERFUME

He was getting married
She came with an arrogant air
smelling of fruit and sweat

He could never buy a perfume for his wife again

NOT A POEM

While poets were torn up
walking between his and she
dramatists kept on hiking for the mid-month date
and the erudite sucked up a pedantic gigolo
comically,
four lines found a couple-spectacle.

FROM ABIGAIL'S EYES

She answered all his letters with resolute passion
He could not love back
guess,
love is the unanswered.

We don't know rain from a fountain
never did.

JENNY

She could have been just about anything,
but she chose to be sad.

Jenny is my evening tea.

JENNY'S SKY

Jenny could stand on the attic
and draw the sun.
She knew when others would die.
On her coffin, she wrote
it would rain in April again.

Jenny,
she was the sky.

WALKS

I started walking on the college road,
two dogs were sleeping under
she took my little finger

the universe expanded in a jump.

It is not only 'and' that joins a sentence.

CLASS

Whenever 'if' and 'then' fall from 'why'
your friend comes to attend the class.
She slips,
and chalk colours the dust.

CALVES

I think of love

only blue skirts,
pink calves,

some very pink calves.

IF

If
suddenly one night
living the life you've always wanted
beside a humping machine doing eggs
stilettos in abulia
you think of me, the names I called you in between
European lectures of stolid silk

don't think anymore,
I'm still worse off.
You made the right choice.

SOME THINGS

Can you build me a wooden house that will not
break in winter?

Baba has been waiting in my dreams, a kidney in
hand, at the hospital's ground floor.
There are no first floors here,
only slipper steps running in desperation.

Paint your moles sad,
the butterflies are here.

They are watching the stage.

TOWARDS LOVE

Jack was trying to be a bad person,
but he couldn't imagine her nude.

That was probably love
or something around that quarter.

STORY

Let me tell you a story
where writing ain't up to talking,
and talking can't walk too.

Her lips can't say the kiss,
and the kiss isn't trembling.

Let me tell you a story where
we try to talk
but can't because that's how

it was supposed to be
and that happens in fairy tales.

Only they edit it well.

SHE AND THE POET

The poet was sitting on a pole.
She
on a blue tapered seat.

The poet didn't write;
because
it was her.

The poet was nude;
because
she wore him.

The poet,
it was her.

BUS SIGHTS

If it hadn't rained,
we wouldn't have taken the bus
where she sat
in conjugal distress looking for safety
a ten-rupee ticket on the highroad
ain't much sexy;
we stood at an Olympic-bar length and did it.

While all the passengers
got down at bus-stops
we succumbed to human presence.
We had only seen each other from a distance.

OEDIPUS, MY FRIEND

Sit in a bus
with obvious intentions
of moving out or in, the least you
expect is a size battle.
A man with a belly, longer and bigger
than adjectives' alibi
was brushing his man mountain against a boy hand.

They both tried to imagine length,
she
looking prim in oyster ads knew
it did not matter.

The boy could be Oedipus, my friend.

ABIGAIL THROUGH A LENS

She had hair flowing back into Alice's Wonderland,
and lips telling stories about the birth of loneliness
they were in love for fifty-seven seconds.
As she was dressing up like a doll on her thirtieth birthday,
he gifted her
the last three seconds.

Her hubby never saw her lipstick again.

ABIGAIL'S

It is easy to pause and
block the person you had loved.

Secretly, in difference

but in a pub when they begin strumming
a 90s classic in serene blue, or
a new lyric of love undone looks sideways,
with necks smelling of cologne, a touch of
meaty aesthetics in black
all the undone and the doing

remind me
of you

and I think with regular failure,

I could go through it all
even if we were only young hormones.

ABIGAIL AND LOVE

Dear Abigail,

We understood each other's fighting words very well
at least had that till the end. Now,
they don't understand my words.
I don't know when I fight
and when I think.

To them,
it is all the same

as I am growing old,
I see love as the friction
between two mostly similar rubbers
than a lullaby made of sugar.

SHE RETURNS

I see you, Abigail

through the windows of distress
wearing pink and white.
Place your palms on the green catafalque,
bite into the bier, darling!
String the dead!

LOW BLOW

She was happy cause it rained hard
smug in her couch, she could read
how Victorians took a spank
flanking a mushy orgasm on the wall.

She was on the tropical bus
lodged into negligence and horse-pumped equality
muttering one line into a thought

a tomato can show you that equality is a blind bullet.

GIBBERISH

I want to touch her face
tell her I care
I don't need to kiss her nipples
to show my need
I can walk away perfectly well
but I want to gently kiss her temple
May be even the bottled nose
not further down
I told her all this
in a sunny cemetery
she said two things I vividly remember
One, she wants me to teach her Eliot and
if kissing her would make me fall
Perhaps, I did not construct the sentence well

I visit the cemetery often, not why you think I do
that is if you've followed the first paragraph.
It tells me tales, lavender pages
Born
and
dying
into life
I cannot construct sentences
Well, I cannot

IMPORTANT THINGS

I always wrote about love
falling in, dripping out, the other one falling;
studied its mitochondria.

That's past like the green light of a gigolo.
Now, I study dustbins, bagpipers,
and other
Important Things.

REVERIE

The fan still revolves with the light from crevices
the only neon in the room is the LED blur
from defunct phones
I remember you
after innumerable testosterone exhaustions.
Holmes knocks on the door,
I can't convince him—
"I am not the shrinking assistant!"

Black chairs hop about the room in protest.
Some antic songs testify in my defence—
"The poets are all sleeping!"

Holmes leaves, leaving the door ajar.
The neon blows out.
My crevices light the room blue.
We were sparrows, pal.
I don't remember anything else.

GOLD

I had put all my empathy into a bag of gold,
forgetting that in every life
I had
jumped in the river,
and died without air.

DEAR JOSEPH

Joseph, my favourite colour is black.
I have tattoos all over me;
one on my shoulder,
another on my abdomen,
and the last one on my hips.

You stand out in class, Joseph!
The white shirt
loosely fits your apex frame.
Some words have made me fumble in the past,
but you
you're just a man!

They come in neat kurtas.
Lit
by paint around their lips.
Curls
bouncing with consumption's choir.
My tee
falls short of metal chords.
You
you don't hear me as often.

Poetry is a universe of pristine chaos,
I've
seen you write in class.
Down
with your ball-point
scratching for light, almost!
We are not very rich, you should know.

Yesterday, I got your name
orientations of gender crossed us
in corridors that smell of burnt caffeine
we
flirted with tobacco and condensed milk.

We'll meet six months later, Joseph.
Till then, keep that shirt clean.

A CARNIVAL AND THEM

The hands of the poet
touched her

under the table
scratched a poem.
From a very far land,
sounds of the Carnival peeped in,
he plunged in her moonlit hair,
till breath found way.
They centred on bodies of dead stars
Bakhtin on the left,
Right had Hamlet.
The night was
carnivorous.

A SUNDAY MORNING

Diving into lanes, I find infinity. I come upon
a thing I had treasured
oblivion

Sun pouring out through the window
I see dad in his loose white vest
I smell his local perfume.
He wakes up, walks to the market
I see him returning with bags.

Ma starts cooking,
the aroma of seeds
on the table, fried stuff
Baba had bought those as brunch.
I called them names then
I don't remember.

From old copies, I treasure inklings.
Inklings of first love, heartbreaks
scribbles, young verses
penned in nativity.

Time takes my hand

I walk some more.
She brings me to that afternoon
lunch, spread on the table.
White things, a bit of flesh, red.
I know only water
yet, I see myself
not drinking
Ma's beliefs to help digestion
I remember, vague, very vague.

Sky turns orange, pale
but
Baba comes up, stories I hear
of generations, inheritance
familial ties, virtues, values
Gifts me flowers.
Ma's melodies I hear
blissful, so serene
Do I know a word?

At night
we three
sleep.
No not just lie
I sleep, beside me
The nubile me
Ma Baba.

You may not like this
I know it is boring.
Don't read it.
I love it already
it was something,
a Sunday morning.

ON READING BOLANO

As I met her two hundred and fifty years
after a long hibernated kiss
she seemed freckled with ink
marks all over her body.

She was reading Gide
and talking about rights to an older woman,
who seemed delightfully aloof.

While I overheard the conversation,
she met my mole with a glance
and smiled.
We walked back, a little upward from the sky
and did not feel the cold of the universe.

Kissing again,
I told her
this time,
I will not be aloof like the woman.

ALONE

I miss not being alone.
Loneliness was alone
it bought a boat.

Alone was lonely
it sailed away.

WHO AM I?

I am a bunch of hormones
five prescribed aspirins,
a cheat meal and cold coffee in a bag of
two large sized balls.

I'm oversized morality
and the fear of everything in nothing of
more than five inches.
I'm a bit of a rabbit's pillow cover
but you
you can be a pen knife who is friends with the sun.

WHY ARE WE NEVER ONE?

After twenty five years of marriage,
man asked his wife
'Why are we never one?'

Wife looked back,
'Because you love the lights!'
'What?'

'Exactly, he would have understood.'

FOR KIDS

I see kids around me
with so much hope
about love
songs, poems
more songs
waiting for video calls
whatsapp messages
calls, endless calls
defeating the night's purpose
I want to tell
them
my stories of sms days, recharging with eleven rupee packs
waiting for that one woman for years and years
and then see her not love you, which is okay
but not respect you, not treat you as a human being
other women who were treated the same by other men
doors closing only to violence and blood
lust and lost kindness
I try to tell them all those songs are nothing
but the culture's fancy
lies told
as are told to toddlers.

Nobody will tell them
that there is no love,
no lovers in the end
your need has to be to find someone
who will at least be kind to others
even if not to you.

I cannot tell them all of it is a fucking lie
you cannot erase the hope of love
and I guess
that is human.

I'LL BE FREE

while living a successful life
with success on both sides of your rubber throne
and sulphur in your moist, cooled air
when you'll think of me like
the wolf remembers a mountain

know
that I am still free
know
that even if chains entangle me,
I am still indifferent
as indifferent I was
about our love, our marriage, our children
know
that I am hungry
unsuccessful
travelling in public transport
yet far from the public
I am residing
in the mountains
like an indifferent hermit on a rainy night
under a starry skybed

or
a warrior lying in a starless ravine

yet know,
that I am still free

BEFORE TOMORROW

A small room
the man on the bed
after a day's work in inertia
while,
the woman was staring at the colourful screen
they call television.
Not a word
No breeze
No rain for eight months.
The spirit of the mother laughed nearby
they thought they heard her
but ignored
amongst the voices coming from the painted glass

Tomorrow
a smaller room, a shorter man, a paler woman, and
A bigger screen

between us!

SPACES

One word
two words
spaces
more spaces.

They found
nostalgia, disease, and finally
committed
matricide for insurance.
Both were my aunts.

SPARROWS

When you grow old but still look
firm, and sparrows are your only friend
you feel insipid growth
but what about people who were not born in the mountains,
never lived there but been there all along
If you read the long line, you're like them.
Old as the wine that was born when we still
made love. You've reared sheep
and ate ice and not known what
nerves are
used words like an octogenarian in forms
and poems while dying with prostatitis
and needles of genitalia. When you grow old,
growing dies and habits become moist.
You may wait for a telephone ring or a ping but you get
sparrows as your only friends.

ESTRANGEMENT

She left

because
he believed love
was about letting go

TEA

Come, kiss me
for I have been kissing bottle caps all night
I promise I'd not want you to stay
or sit by me when I'm alone.
Kiss
and we'll forget each other.
You will really, and I will
pretend to.
When you return home tonight
and find your coffee table sad, remember
how it affects your nerves, makes you fall
in love. Drink some dry tea may be
with exotic flavours created from
despair
and then when you'll kiss me,
I'll stop drinking tea.
We will forget each other.
You will, really. I will
pretend to.

MEDIOCRITY

The best lines are edited by the mediocre
to become the worst.
An experience is reduced to an analogy
and
anything that requires thinking is rejected
as complex.
Towards visuals they run but are caught by ill-love
an un-poetic

ill-love

for

un-knowledge.

So the worst is established as a standard
while lines above are known as a poem.

MIDNIGHT

It's 2 am.
You are watching a random web series
not taking calls, preparing for a retreat
suddenly a pregnant woman
looks exactly like the girl you first fell in love with
you feel
a weird desire of wanting to see her 18-year-old eyes
laced with mascara and naughty laughter
that imperfect nose which made you paint
underwear
three words later, she became somebody's mom
and five years before
somebody's wife.
It is 2:08 am
not just a web series
not just another poem.

JACK

Jack was trying to be a bad person,
but he couldn't imagine her nude.
That was probably love,
or something around that quarter.

FAMILY

He was alive even after the suicide that
the media kept chiming about
alive, even later
when all the arrangements of soul travel was complete
he thought he could do some good
but couldn't grip afterlife.
He was alive through numerous discussions and heartbreaks
in rooms where nobody thought he lived
he heard all the good about him for the first week
thereafter, he walked amongst lips of negative feedback

on some days,
he was God—called upon to interfere
with happenings around the sun
and during other days,
he was an example of what not to be, whom not to follow
he was the shortcut-taker, heavily derided over coffee.

He was alive long after all this
the suicide did not kill him
but then his family came casually singing about his failure.
He was not alive long after that.

He died.

FALLING

She
doesn't stop peeping.
We do not stop playing with
all the tools of a closed window
in social media.
I do not know if she is,
but I am falling in love
again
not with the playing
but with the freaky pulse rate
she induces into my rational existence,
into my irrational writing.

ORGAN

Every night I build a man,
a faceless organ and use it on other organs
hide the face behind the organ
but the organ is soft
softer than my virile face
so it can never match up.
While the organ reverses its role,
the face falls off on the virtual typing
and
runs away.

I stay locked all night in my organ.
A face in the dried dark.

MORNINGS

she was happy outside the house
laughing with all the colors on her dress
clicking photos and hanging out;
her dates always ended with the boy calling her
so it was, undoubtedly, a successful life

she cried every night sleeping on the nervous couch
the bed was always tidy
like her mornings

UN-REAL

It took me some time to understand that LinkedIn
is not the real world.
The real world is where it rains, drains are clogged,
houses are destroyed by cyclones, people die
people are born
lovers meet
pandemics thrive, vaccines are made.

It took me some time to know
that the real world is more pain
less jealousy, more hate
less insecurity, more loss
less love. It is where lovers do not meet anymore,
it only rains.

LONELINESS

it is not the loneliness that kills you
it is what you've known about loneliness
that it is a frisky cat which will leave you,
when it doesn't
and comes back
scratching on the glass with pink claws,
you
do not think about children in schools,
couples in prison, and parents
in living rooms.
"You, only you are lonely", the cat says.

you
believe it like you believed in love,
in war, in heroes, and
then it is you and the cat, every night
the cat ain't lonely
it's you, only you

CONVERSATION

A conversation between a staircase and a window can begin in any which way you imagine but they will always talk about sunshine.

They both came to me remembering how everyone treats them—scratching or thumping flakes off them.

The Staircase is sombre, wise, knows a thing or two about people leaving; often, quite often in haste.

The Window is younger, jubilant, almost gay as it is more closer to the idea of staying. It doesn't mind the sunset; hopeful, that a sunrise is hours away.

Staircase, who is very close to me, is picky about sunshine. It has seen damp days, times of stumbling inertia.

The maid tells me how both are clueless, unapologetic and messy. I think how different they are and that it belies a very humane disposition to use the same adjectives for both. The maid, on such days, reminds me of my peers.

It is good to be living in a non-living world.

AMNESIA

with memories working against us
amnesia is our hope
because if we forget each other
I will fall for you
and you'll pretend not to

KISSES

some kisses end with flowers
some
move down to bear-hugs

digging up glances

DREAMS

When the light goes out,
people sleep.
I come out for you
to breathe you in, like we used to
in dreams.
Dreams that I don't have
anymore.

LONELY

when you are alone
stay alone

talking to people will
make you lonely

and then
you won't be unable to bear alone

making you

lonelier

ADIEU

A peep down

Side by side

A stick
Metro-rail

This city
At world's end

Conscious

Very conscious

Adieu

Rit Chattapadhyay holds first-class postgraduate and M.Phil degrees from the University of Calcutta. His M.Phil research focused on the evolution of Edward Bond's drama from the 1960s to the new millennium. His poem 'Letter to Abigail' has been published in *Kaafiyana* by Readomania; 'Knowing Love' has been published in *The Significant Anthology* by Morph Books; and 'Phulboni' has been published in an anthology titled *Cologne of Heritage: Incredible Bengal* by Vishwabharati Research Centre. Chattapadhyay works in the capacity of a Guest Faculty at the Department of English, Sanskrit College and University. He has also worked as a Lecturer at the Postgraduate Department of English, Maulana Azad College, and Postgraduate Department of English, Bethune College. He has taught core courses on Romantic and Victorian Literature, History of the English Language, Indian Classical Theatre, and elective courses on Theatre Studies. Chattapadhyay is also a Specialist Academic Editor at Cactus Communications for over two years.